BOOKWORMS

Just the Opposite
Up / Down

Exactamente lo opuesto
Arriba / Abajo

SPANISH
J
153.7
GOR

Sharon Gordon

Marshall Cavendish
Benchmark
New York

The kite is up.

❖

La cometa está arriba.

The kite is down.

La cometa está abajo.

The dog is up.

El perro está arriba.

The dog is down.

El perro está abajo.

The ball is up.

La pelota está arriba.

The ball is down.

❖

La pelota está abajo.

The cat is up.

El gato está arriba.

The cat is down.

El gato está abajo.

The girl is up.

La niña está arriba.

The girl is down.

❖

La niña está abajo.

The frog is up.

La rana está arriba.

The frog is down.

---❖---

La rana está abajo.

The balloon is up.

❖

El globo está arriba.

The balloon is down.

❖

El globo está abajo.

The seesaw is up.

El subibaja está arriba.

The seesaw is down.

El subibaja está abajo.

The boy is up.

El niño está arriba.

Come down!

❖

¡Bájate ya!

Words We Know
Palabras que sabemos

ball
pelota

ballon
globo

boy
niño

cat
gato

dog
perro

frog
rana

girl
niña

kite
cometa

seesaw
subibaja

21

Index

Índice

About the Author
Datos biográficos de la autora

Sharon Gordon has written many books for young children. She has always worked as an editor. Sharon and her husband Bruce have three children, Douglas, Katie, and Laura, and one spoiled pooch, Samantha. They live in Midland Park, New Jersey.

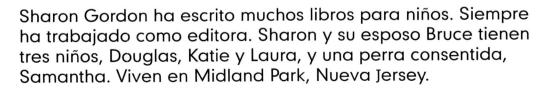

Sharon Gordon ha escrito muchos libros para niños. Siempre ha trabajado como editora. Sharon y su esposo Bruce tienen tres niños, Douglas, Katie y Laura, y una perra consentida, Samantha. Viven en Midland Park, Nueva Jersey.

With thanks to Nanci Vargus, Ed.D. and Beth Walker Gambro, reading consultants

Marshall Cavendish Benchmark
99 White Plains Road
Tarrytown, New York 10591-9001
www.marshallcavendish.us

Library of Congress Cataloging-in-Publication Data

Gordon, Sharon.
[Up down. Spanish & English]
Up down = Arriba abajo / Sharon Gordon. — Bilingual ed.
p. cm. — (Bookworms. Just the opposite = Exactamente lo opuesto)
Includes index.
ISBN-13: 978-0-7614-2449-9 (bilingual ed.)
ISBN-10: 0-7614-2449-0 (bilingual ed.)
ISBN-13: 978-0-7614-2369-0 (Spanish edition)
ISBN-10: 0-7614-1573-4 (English edition)
1. Space perception—Juvenile literature. I. Title. II. Title: Arriba abajo.
III. Series: Gordon, Sharon. Bookworms. Just the opposite (Spanish & English)

BF469.G6718 2006b
153.7'52—dc22
2006017351

Spanish Translation and Text Composition by Victory Productions, Inc.
www.victoryprd.com

Photo Research by Anne Burns Images

Cover Photos: *Corbis*: (up-Royalty Free), (down-Tim Davis)
The photographs in this book are used with permission and through the courtesy of: *Photri, Inc.*: pp. 1 (left), 4 Wachter; pp. 1 (right), 5, 20 (bottom right) Bonnie Sue Ranch; pp. 2, 3, 21 (top right) Fotopic; p. 6 James Kirby; pp. 7, 20 (top left) Brian Drake. *Corbis*: pp. 8, 10, 21 (bottom left) Royalty Free; pp. 9, 20 (bottom middle) Tim Davis; p. 11 Cat Gwynn; pp. 14, 20 (bottom left) Paul A. Souders; p. 15 Bosco Laura/Sygma; pp. 18, 20 (top right) Laura Doss. *Animals Animals*: pp. 12, 13, 21 (top left) Stephen Dalton. *Photo Edit*: pp. 16, 17, 21 (bottom right) Myrleen Ferguson Cate. *SWA Photo*: p. 19.

Series design by Becky Terhune

Printed in Malaysia
1 3 5 6 4 2